Small Town

Pamela McDowell

LET'S READ
AV²
BY WEIGL™
ADDED VALUE • AUDIO VISUAL

Go to **www.av2books.com**, and enter this book's unique code.

BOOK CODE

T686734

AV² by Weigl brings you media enhanced books that support active learning.

AV² provides enriched content that supplements and complements this book. Weigl's AV² books strive to create inspired learning and engage young minds in a total learning experience.

Your AV² Media Enhanced books come alive with...

Audio
Listen to sections of the book read aloud.

Video
Watch informative video clips.

Embedded Weblinks
Gain additional information for research.

Try This!
Complete activities and hands-on experiments.

Key Words
Study vocabulary, and complete a matching word activity.

Quizzes
Test your knowledge.

Slide Show
View images and captions, and prepare a presentation.

... and much, much more!

Published by AV² by Weigl
350 5th Avenue, 59th Floor New York, NY 10118
Website: www.av2books.com

Library of Congress Cataloging-in-Publication Data

McDowell, Pamela.
 Small town / Pamela McDowell.
    pages cm. -- (Where do you live?)
Includes index.
ISBN 978-1-4896-3613-3 (hard cover : alk. paper) -- ISBN 978-1-4896-3614-0 (soft cover : alk. paper) --
ISBN 978-1-4896-3615-7 (single user ebk.) -- ISBN 978-1-4896-3616-4 (multi-user ebk.)
1. Cities and towns--Juvenile literature. 2. City and town life--Juvenile literature. 3. Country life--Juvenile literature. I. Title.
HT152.M36 2016
307.76--dc23
                                        2015014087

Printed in the United States of America in Brainerd, Minnesota
1 2 3 4 5 6 7 8 9 0 19 18 17 16 15

072015
072415

Project Coordinator: Jared Siemens
Design: Mandy Christiansen

The publisher acknowledges Alamy, Corbis Images, Getty Images, and iStock as the primary image suppliers for this title.

Small Town

CONTENTS

I live in a small town.

A few thousand people live in my town.

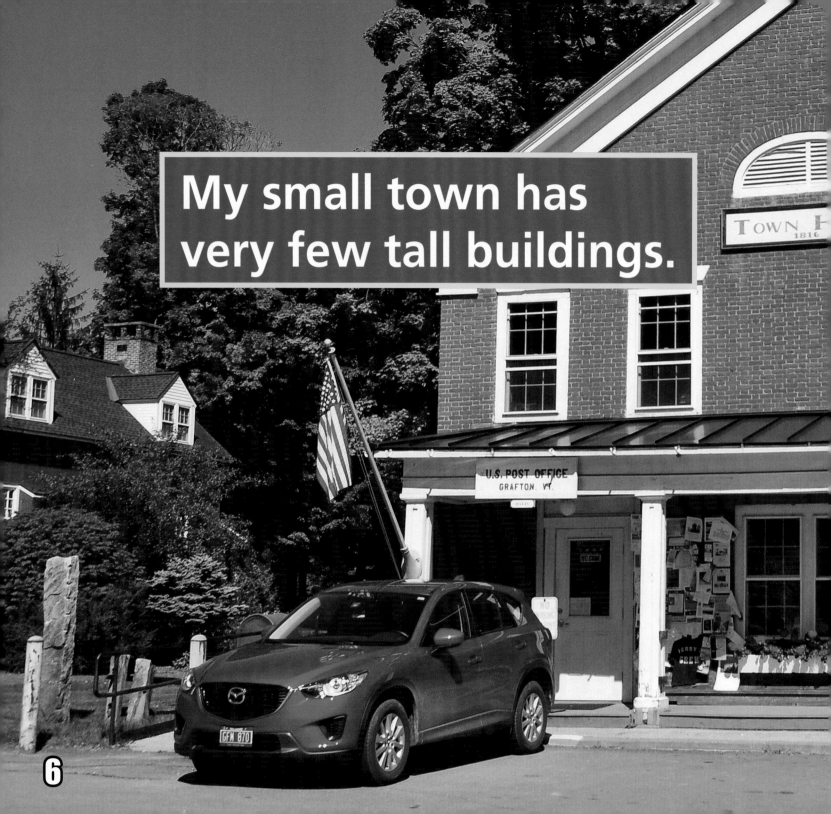

My small town has very few tall buildings.

The biggest building is the town hall. There is an American flag at the town hall.

My home is near the edge of town. We have a large yard with grass and trees.

When I look out my window, I can see my friend's house.

My town has one school. I walk to school every day with my friends.

My friends and I play hopscotch during recess.

People often walk
to where they need to go.

They do not need to drive because places are very close together.

Main street is the center of my town. Almost all of the places to eat, work, and shop are here.

There is a parade on main street on holidays.

Farmers bring fresh fruits and vegetables to the market in my town.

My favorite food is watermelon.

My small town has fun places to go and things to do. I like to ride bikes with my friends.

Our favorite place
to go is the library.

The people in my town decide who will be the leader of our town.

POLLING PLACE
投票站 CASILLA ELECTORAL
投票所 LUGAR NG BOTOHAN
투표소 PHÒNG PHIẾU

The leader is called the mayor. The mayor works at the town hall.

Which of these places looks most like the place where you live?

What is the same?
What is different?

THE SHIP INN

Sarah Louise

WH256

MR 3

MR 3

NIL DESPERANDUM

Quarter Bell
WH 425

KEY WORDS

Research has shown that as much as 65 percent of all written material published in English is made up of 300 words. These 300 words cannot be taught using pictures or learned by sounding them out. They must be recognized by sight. This book contains 63 common sight words to help young readers improve their reading fluency and comprehension. This book also teaches young readers several important content words, such as proper nouns. These words are paired with pictures to aid in learning and improve understanding.

Page	Sight Words First Appearance
4	a, I, in, live, small
5	few, my, people
6	has, very
7	American, an, at, is, the, there
8	and, have, home, large, near, of, trees, we, with
9	can, house, look, out, see, when
10	day, every, one, school, to, walk
11	play
12	go, need, often, they, where
13	are, because, close, do, not, places, together
14	all, almost, eat, here, work
15	on
17	food
18	like, things
19	our
20	be, who, will

Page	Content Words First Appearance
4	small town
6	buildings
7	flag, town hall
8	edge, grass, yard
9	friend, window
11	hopscotch, recess
14	center, main street
15	holidays, parade
16	farmers, fruits, market, vegetables
17	watermelon
18	bikes
19	library
20	leader
21	mayor

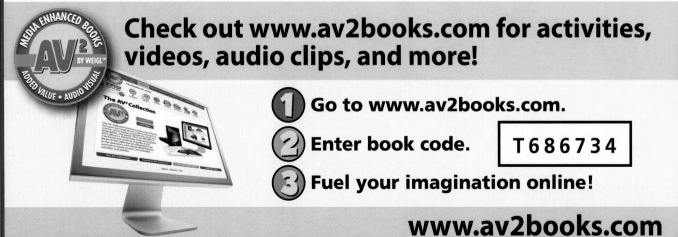

Check out www.av2books.com for activities, videos, audio clips, and more!

1 Go to www.av2books.com.

2 Enter book code. `T 6 8 6 7 3 4`

3 Fuel your imagination online!

www.av2books.com